GLORY MAGNITUDE

GLORY MAGNITUDE

Alicia Marie Hopkins

Copyright © 2006 by Alicia Marie Hopkins.

Library of Congress Control Number:		2006904130
ISBN 10:	Hardcover	1-4257-1622-9
	Softcover	1-4257-1623-7
ISBN 13:	Hardcover	978-1-4257-1622-6
	Softcover	978-1-4257-1623-3

All rights reserved. No part of this book may be reproduced or transmitted in any form or by any means, electronic or mechanical, including photocopying, recording, or by any information storage and retrieval system, without permission in writing from the copyright owner.

Scripture taken from the HOLY BIBLE, NEW INTERNATIONAL VERSION ®. Copyright 1973, 1978, 1984 by International Bible Society. Used by permission of Zondervan. All rights reserved.

Scripture quotations marked (NLT) are taken from the Holy Bible, New Living Translation, Copyright © 1996. Used by permission of Tyndale House Publishers, Inc., Wheaton, Illinois 60189. All rights reserved.

Scripture taken form the New King James Version. Copyright © 1979, 1980, 1982 by The Nelson, Inc. Used by permission. All rights reserved.

This book was printed in the United States of America.

To order additional copies of this book, contact:
Xlibris Corporation
1-888-795-4274
www.Xlibris.com
Orders@Xlibris.com
34198

CONTENTS

In the Presence of Glory Magnitude 9
Section I Prayer 11
On Your Knees 12
Hearing My Father 14
Revive This World Oh Sweet Jesus! 15
Section II Faith 16
Faith 17
Come Follow Me 18
Standing Your Ground 19
Have a little faith 20
No one ever said Walking on Water was Fun 21
Going Forward 22
Father 24
Believing is More Than Anything Else 25
Determination 26
Impossible Isn't a Real Word 27
Section III. Devotion 28
Treasure I Need You 29
Jesus I Need You 30
All You Can Do Is Pray 31
Don't Forget 32
I Am What I Am 33
Section IV Life 35
To Live 36
Invitation of Salvation 37
Purposes of Life 39
Who Am I 40
The Uncomfortable Zone 42
Nothing lasts forever 43
I Know You Are There For Me 44
The River of Hope 45
A Walk Down Memory Lane 46
Section V Worship 47
David 48

Dancing With My King 49
Worshippers Don't Belong in Pews 50
Lights on the Dance Floor 51
Section VI Thanksgiving 52
Savior 53
Forgiven 54
Hallelujah Freedom Is my Friend 55
Section VII Friendship 56
A Friend 57
Friends until the End 58
Friendships 59
Saying I Love You 60
My Child 61
Counselor 62
Our Father Is All Around 63
The Greatest Gift Of All 64
The Man Who Sits Everywhere 65
Yesterday's Mark 66
Section VIII Random Poetry 67
Days of Relevance 68
Heaven's in the sky 69

I dedicate this book first and foremost to my savior and my king Jesus Christ. I would also like to dedicate this book to my family, friends, professors, colleagues, and those who have helped me become the person I am today.

I would like to give a special thanks to the following

Mr. Leopard-My seventh grade literature teacher
Mr. Cooper-My eighth grade English teacher
Derrick Rigg
Holly Wingrove
Katie Snyder
Joshua Hopkins—My brother

In the Presence of Glory Magnitude

In his presence
Walking around
Not knowing what to do
Not knowing what to say

In his presence
The quiet stillness of the air
The quiet motionless feeling
The silence has not yet been broken

In his presence
Down on your knees
With your face on the floor
Weeping before the king

In his presence
There is light shinning
It's his glory magnitude
Right before our very eyes

In his presence
The flood waters open up
It's his every lasting love
Just flooding and filling the room

In his presence
The sick and oppressed are healed
And their pain is covered in his blood

In his presence
The cross and a sign flashing
With the words forgiven are in the midst

In his presence
An abundant joy fills
Every creature all over creation

In his presence
God's wonders happen
But even more so
You've surrendered your all
and now you have seen his glory magnitude

Section I Prayer

Matthew 7:7-8
Keep on asking and you will be given what you ask for
Keep on looking and you find
Keep on knocking and the door will be opened
For everyone who asks receives and
Everyone who seeks finds and the door is open to everyone who knocks (NLT)

Matthew 21:22
If you believe you will receive everything you ask for in prayer (NLT)

John 15:7
But if you stay joined to me, and my words remain in you, you may ask any request you like and it will be granted (NLT)

Mark 11:24
Listen to me, you can pray about anything, if you believe you will have it. (NLT)

On Your Knees

On your knees
Crying out
With your face on the floor
No distraction
You and God
Face to face

Giving you a heads up
To what's around you
Giving you a choice
For what's ahead of you
Giving you a sign
To see you will be okay
Giving you all you need
To believe

On your knees
Crying out
Asking for second chance
Because you know you've screwed up
A time or two

On your knees he speaks to you
This time it's not just in words
But in pictures too

He shows you a flood
Of his everlasting love
He shows you a cross
With the words forgiven in front of it
He shows you a door
And he says it's your choice
And he says it can be yours, if you just let it
He shows you so much more
But in time he leaves you with these words

I know the plans I have for you
It's your job to trust in me
And the steps are sure to follow
There may be times of test and trial
But I will be there in everything

Your heart is mine
It always will be
If you let it

On your knees
You will see
Life isn't how it's meant to be
It's what I want it to be

Hearing My Father

So many times you bless us with
Your awesome miracles
And we forget to say a blessing back

So many times we hear you calling our name
But we sometimes ignore you

So many times we hear you tell us things
But yet we still ignore you
And do what we want to do

Time passes by so quickly
And people tend to forget
How to hear the Lord

Revive This World Oh Sweet Jesus!

It's crazy how we live in a world
That can be so messed up sometimes
Oh sweet Jesus
This world needs you
I cry out for those who can't
And pray for those who won't
Lord this world can seem so empty at times
We need your amazing love to fill this bouncy ball shaped world
For your son died on that cross
He bares the pain that no man
Can ever endure
He sets people free
Even those who think they are lost
But with Jesus they are found
He knows what will happen in the end
He's the only one who can change this crazy world of ours

Section II Faith

James 1:5-6
If any of you lacks wisdom, he should ask God, who gives generously to all without finding fault, and it will be given to him. But when he asks, he must believe and not doubt, because he who doubts is like a wave of the sea, blown and tossed by the wind. (NIV)

Hebrews 11:1
Now faith is being sure of what we hope for and certain of what we do not see. (NIV)

Hebrews 11:6
And without faith it is impossible to please God, because anyone who comes to him must believe that he exists and that he rewards those who earnestly seek him. (NIV)

Faith

When everyone discourages you
But you still believe that all things are possible
When the world spins you in a million and one directions
And you're still holding on with your all
When everyone thinks your going to fall
But you just keep going striving towards that goal
When everyone is against you
And you know that God is there for you always
When life isn't the way you want it to be
And you're still praising the Lord for being alive
When you don't get what you want in life
And you're still thanking the Lord for everything
When you feel so weak
But you can acknowledge that God is your strength
When all is said, and done
And you haven't given up yet, that's when you know its faith

Come Follow Me

Out far in the desert
Lies an old man
Watching and waiting
To see if anyone finds him
To see if anyone knows he's alive
But he knows God knows he's alive
So he prays
Then a boy walks out of nowhere
And says come follow me

* This poem is an earlier writing written in the late 1990's.

Standing Your Ground

It's not about the meetings you have
Or the many celebrations you have
It's not about whose up in front speaking
It's not about the band, or the worship team

It's about you and God
Face to face
It's about the interaction with you and God
It's about being in his presence
It's about hearing from God
And hearing his voice

It's about being alone with the Father
All the time,
Not just in church
Not just to please anyone
But it's about you and God all the time

It's about having a relationship
One on one
Twenty four seven
Even when friends don't believe in him
It's about standing you ground
Sharing your faith
Twenty four seven
And believing God can change the world

Have A Little Faith

When your going through
The hard times
Have a little faith

Don't give up
Keep going and try your hardest
To make the best of what you can

It won't be easy
It won't be hard
It will just be a challenge
But you can do anything
If you just believe

No one ever said Walking on Water was Fun

Everyday in everyway
God shows us things
Sometimes they are perfect
Other times they are not
But in everything God has a plan

A plan that will work in time
But in that there will be tests and trials
To see if we will keep our faith
One thing we have to remember is
God will never give us more than we can handle

Sometimes a little can seem like a lot
But God knows what will happen
We just have to seek him and believe
Even if it means
Getting down on our knees
And getting down on our face
And asking God for help

No one ever said
Walking on water was the easiest thing to do
But with God's help
The time, tests, and trials are worth it
If we have faith

Going Forward

I look back at yesterday
And I remember what it was like
All the times I just wanted to run away
And knew I couldn't stay
All the times I wanted to cry
But never did because it just wasn't the thing to do
All the times I called out to the Lord
And didn't realize he was right beside me
All the times I was in a pit
And I just wanted to quit

I can look back at all these things
And I can sit here and dwell or
I can choose right now to move on
And put them in the past
And trust God with my life

Indeed that's what I've done
My life is in the Father's hands
I'm resting in his arms
And I know that he is my freedom

I'm bound no more by demonic things
I'm bound no more by chains
I'm bound no more by steel

I'm free
Free to dance
Free to sing
Free to worship
Free to cry
Free to shout
Free to praise the Lord
My freedom is from the Lord
And him alone

I'm in a period where God
Is restoring me, healing me
And showing me my life

My freedom is yours oh Lord
And I thank-you

Father

Run to Him
He will be there
With his arms
Wide open
He will be there
Waiting to hold you in his arms
Waiting to tell you
That he loves you
He will be there
Standing his ground
Waiting for you to just receive
All that he has for you
He will be there
To offer you a gift
If you will just accept it
And receive it
He will be there to comfort
And to care for you
He knows your every need
Before you even ask

Believing is More Than Anything Else

I see you every morning
When you wake up
I'm your strength when you are weak
I am your food
When you are hungry
Just grab a bite to eat out of my word
I am your water
When you are thirsty
Come to me my child and I will fill your cup
I am your encouragement
When you feel discouraged
And can't take it anymore

I am your words of wisdom
When that friend needs council
I am your daily bread
When you sit down to eat
Or you just need something
I am your tears
When you have the urge to cry
But always Jesus Wept and so can you

I am all of these things and more
Open your eyes my child
I believe in you
You wouldn't be where you are
Without me

Don't give up
But put your hope and joy in me
And more is what you will see

Determination

When everyone around you tells you to give up
That things aren't worth
The fight
It's just a one-way battle
And it's not worth your while
But you continue
On that path you are on
Because you know
That you can make it passed
That stage in your life

Determination is a big word
But if you truly look at the meaning of it
And think of it as more than just a word
But as a pathway for change
Then there's power in it

If you keep going and fight through the strongholds and words
Things will get better
Things will change.
If you don't give up
But hold fast
To those things that you believe in
Then everything will work out

Impossible Isn't a Real Word

Don't let anyone discourage you
Or tell you that you can't do something
Because you are poor
Or because you are too young
With God
Nothing is impossible
We don't have to waste our time
Putting up speed limit signs
All we can do
Is trust and believe
God can make anything happen
It's only a matter of time

Section III. Devotion

Hebrews 11:6
And without faith it is impossible to please God, because anyone who comes to him must believe that he exists and that he rewards those who earnestly seek him. (NIV)

Lamentations 3:25
The LORD is good to those whose hope is in him, to the one who seeks him; (NIV)

Jeremiah 29:13
You will seek me and find me when you seek me with all your heart. (NIV)

Deuteronomy 4:29
But if from there you seek the LORD your God, you will find him if you look for him with all your heart and with all your soul. (NIV)

Treasure I Need You

He said you would be somebody
He said you would be something
It's your choice to believe in him
He's that somebody
He's that something
He wants your life hand in hand
He doesn't want half the slice of the pie
He wants the whole thing

It's your choice
Do you want to be somebody?
It's your choice
Don't you want to be something?
It's your choice
It's your decision
It's your vote
So are you in?

It's either you choose now
Because if you wait the offer
Might not still stand
I'm offering you my everything my child
Take it from my hands
Before it's too late
I'm a treasure that no one can live without

Jesus I Need You

I can listen to all these songs
On the radio
About loving you
And searching for you
But until I truly look beyond
The music
The melody
And the beat
I will never see
The real deal
Jesus I need you
I lay myself down to you
I push the things of the world aside
And I cry out to you
Oh Lord
I place my needs before my wants
For I am not joking
Jesus I need you
Not just for a moment
But forever

All You Can Do Is Pray

The world is full of so much hate
I wish it all would stop
The only thing I can do instead of wishing
Is to pray my day away about it

The world is full of so much violence
From guns in our schools
To who knows what anymore

The world is full of so much violence
Oh! can't you make it stop
The only thing I can do is pray
And let God deal with it all

It makes me sick to see this all
Oh lord please help the world
To change there ways and stop
All the hate, violence, and crime

Don't Forget

Reach out
Go for it
But don't forget
Every race you run
Or everything you compete in
God is with you
He knows the end results
He is the only one who knows
If you will win or loose

Reach out
Go for it
But don't forget
To have a Christ-like attitude in every step
Or in every word
To acknowledge God in all things
To be a good sport, even when you loose out
God is watching your every move
A strike against someone
Is a strike against Him
So watch yourself
And remember life isn't all about competitions
It's about knowing God and going for your dreams

I Am What I Am

I'm not a book
Nor am I a flash light

I'm not just something you turn to
When you need help
I'm not just something you turn on or off
When you need it

I'm not a toy
Nor am I a game

I'm not just something you play with for a while
I'm not just something that gets old after a week or two
I'm not just someone you can play games with
I'm not just something you can win or loose at

I'm not a drinking fountain
Nor a materialistic thing
I'm not just something you take a drink from
When you are thirsty
I'm not just something you worship when you want to
I'm not just something you can throw away
When you are tired of it

I'm not a garbage bin
Nor am I a toilet

I'm not just something you put your garbage in
I'm not just something you can dump in
When you can't hold it in anymore
I'm not just something that can be flushed

It's time you face reality
And see what I really am

I am the God of wisdom
and the truth is in my word
I am the light in the darkness
Everyday in everyway

I am the power tool
That gives you directions
On where to go and what to do
I am the right or wrong answer
But if you choose the right answer
I will show you more

I am the fountain of love and life
I supply you with all of your needs
I am your provider
And here I stand and say
Put away your toys because I am worth more

I am your glory
I am your banner
Now sing your praises to me
And watch your life change

Before I forget
I am your God
And most of all
I am your king
Honor me, first in all things
Don't just come to dump on me

Section IV Life

Psalm 71:17-18
Since my youth, O God, you have taught me, and to this day I declare your marvelous deeds. Even when I am old and gray, do not forsake me, O God, till I declare your power to the next generation, your might to all who are to come. (NIV)

Philippians 1:6
"And I am sure that God, who began the good work within you, will continue his work until it is finally finished on that day when Christ Jesus comes back again." (NLT)

To Live

To live life to the fullest
To run around with your arms open wide
To dance for the king no matter where you are
To dream a little dream and reach for the stars
To walk a mile like its nothing
To travel a distance that goes on forever
To believe in something with all of your heart
To treasure something that is distant
To love another like they love you
To hear a voice inside of you
To see with your eyes the world around you
To hear with your ears from the one no one can compare to
To have a feeling of joy inside of you like no other
To stand at his feet and just praise his name
To not give up when life gets you down
To rise above your situation
To live life to its fullest in every walk of life

Invitation of Salvation

Don't mess with me
Because I'm a Jesus freak
I'll tell you a story
If you promise to pass it on

It's a story of life
See here, this little baby
Was born on Christmas Day
A very very long time ago

Jesus was his name in fact
His father our king
Sacrificed his son on a cross
Why you might ask

To pay a price
For our sins
It wasn't a one time thing
He paid the price for all time

The nails in his hands and feet
The crown of thorns on his head
He hung there on that cross
So we could be forgiven
He paid our price in full

God wants your life
He wants it now
The past is the past
And once you say yes
The past is all erased from his memory
Forgiven is a word that will flash
Across your bulletin board that's in your head

All you have to do is accept him in your heart
Here is your invitation
Accept it and watch
Your life change for the good

God's promises are a great thing
To live by
And once you accept the invitation
You can pass it on to others
Just like I have passed on this story to you

Purposes of Life

Each of us
God has a purpose and a plan for
We may not be the greatest at something
Or we may just want to give up
But the Lord wants us to know
No one is perfect
All have sinned and fallen short of the glory of God
He is there for you if you need a shoulder to cry on
When you're in trouble you can seek him for a solution
You don't have to go searching in places for Answers
You just have to trust in the Lord to find the way
For he is always there
To hold our hand
If you should fall down, he will be there to pick you back up again.
Don't be depressed
If you have a frown
Let the Lord turn it around
Cheer up
The Lord loves you so much
Even if you don't realize it
Don't look back at past mistakes or times of trouble
You're forgiven, don't dwell, and move on
Turn your life around
Don't' think negative, but instead think positive
Your life is guaranteed to change
Just watch
Always remember never give up
The Lord loves you so much

Who Am I

I was sitting in church the other day
Trying to figure out
Who I am
And what I am doing with this life of mine

The preacher got up
And spoke a simple but complex word
At the end
I wanted to stand up
And say amen
But yet I was still searching
The thoughts in my mind
Were all over the place
All I knew was that
My heart was not right

I couldn't stay in the place
I'd always been
I had to pack my bags
And run away
I had to break up the camp scene
For I had to realize
I was not a victim
But more so a survivor
For when I boarded my train
I realized there was no going back
I had to say goodbye to Egypt
And hello to the land of freedom

On the train
I realized
I had Jesus in my heart
What more did I need?

On the train that day
Jesus filled me with his love
And offered me some fruit for eternity

He said to me
Child, the road ahead
Is different from the last
Don't worry or be nervous
Because I am here beside you
In every step you take
I will walk with you

The Uncomfortable Zone

Sometimes we have to be uncomfortable
Or in the exit zone
To realize
That if we want to go somewhere
Or be somebody
We can't live in a parallel world
We have to take off our earthly crowns
Lay beside our masks
And hold fast to our dreams
We cannot say "but" or "why"
But instead
We have to look at the bright side
And ask ourselves
Where we want to go?
And how much are we able to give up
To let God work through us
And yet use us to change the world
How much will we give up?
To change this world
And experience a place
Away from that place
We've always felt comfortable in

Nothing lasts forever

Sometimes everything around us can look bad
But if you think about it
Nothing Lasts Forever
You can be in a place in your life
Where everyone is against you
And to top it off everyone is trying to ruin
The things you attempting to accomplish

You can be in a place in your life
Where the floodwaters are drowning you
And everything is just a mess
And you can't keep head above water

You can be a place
Where life looks peachy at the surface
And in reality it's rotten beneath the peel of it all
And you can't say a word about it

You can be in any place,
But if you look at the big picture
Nothing lasts forever

There is this man
Who you might know
He is a savior and a king

He is your hope
In times of trouble
Or In times of need

He will be there
For you
Just receive

He will help you reach that goal
He will hold your head above the water
And He will help you peel away the hurt and pain
Of yesterday

I Know You Are There For Me

So many times I ran away
So many times I screwed up
So many times I let my pain have its way
So many times I tried to end my life

But in everything you were there
When I couldn't run any farther
When I couldn't hide anymore
When I couldn't cry anymore
When I couldn't end my life

You were there for me
When no one else was
When I felt rejected
When I felt abandoned

You were there for me
When I was sad
When I was in pain
When I was afraid

You were there for me
Every day in every way
And as I walk day by day
I know you are walking beside me

The River of Hope

There's a place I go
When life gets tough
I sit down beside the river
To be with my King
My father and my friend

There's a place I go
When life gets tough
It's a place where I can dance with Jesus
My father and my friend

There's a place I go
When life gets tough
It's a place of refuge from the storms of life
A place of hope, forgiveness, and grace
So many places I can go
But here is where I feel his presence
Where I know my father will always be

A Walk Down Memory Lane

A walk down memory lane
The candle in the window
The breath of fresh air
The surroundings everywhere
The people far off in the distance
The harmonic sounds of music fading in the background
The pleasant smells of chestnuts roasting in the fire
The memories that uphold the past
Live on as memories of life

Section V Worship

Psalm 150:1-6
"Praise the Lord! Praise God in His heavenly dwelling; praise Him in His mighty heaven! Praise Him for His mighty works; praise His unequaled greatness! Praise Him with a blast of the trumpet; praise Him with the lyre and harp! Praise Him with the tambourine and dancing; praise Him with the stringed instruments and flutes! Praise Him with a clash of cymbals; praise him with loud clanging cymbals. Let everything that lives sing praises to the Lord! Praise the Lord!" (NLT)

David

He danced before the Lord
Not worrying about who was
Around him

He danced before the Lord
With all praise
And without any shame

He danced before the Lord
With his head held high
And hope in his heart

He danced before the Lord
With everything instilled inside of him
He praised the Lord

Dancing With My King

I will dance
I will sing
I will give glory to my king

I will shout
I will sing
I will dance before my king

No more chains
No more shackles
Nothing can hold me back now

I will dance
I will sing
I will give glory to my king

No more will the enemy attack me
No more will the chair confine me
I want to dance before my king

No more restrictions
No more limitations
For he is my hands and feet

I will shout
I will sing
I will dance before my king

Worshippers Don't Belong in Pews

There were many songs in my heart
That one Sunday morning
I longed to dance a dance
With my savior and my King
The pastor got up with a word
About a young man we all know
From Bible times
He said
He danced before the Lord
In freedom and humility
As I heard those words
I longed to get up out of my seat
The devil had a plan
Because I was about to sit down
But before I could sit down
The Holy Spirit took hold
God had taken control
I felt the shaking in my body
My heart was exploding with joy
And I was dancing
With my sweet Jesus

Lights on the Dance Floor

He said to me
Daughter come
Take my hand
I have something to show you
He picked me up
Off the ground
He took my hands
And he spun me around
He turned me in circles
Like the earth was slowly spinning
He held me close
So I wouldn't fall down
He gave me strength
To move about
Up and down across the dance floor
My father danced
A dance with me
Until the morning light gave way
And all I could see were beams of light
Heading straight towards me

Section VI Thanksgiving

Psalm 9:1-2
I will thank you, Lord, with all my heart; I will tell of all the marvelous things you have done. I will be filled with joy because of you. I will sing praises to your name, O Most High. (NLT)

Deuteronomy 10:21
"He is your praise; he is your God, who performed for you those great and awesome wonders you saw with your own eyes." (NIV)

Savior

There was a time in life
When I use to think
That there was no hope in life
But then one day
I met Jesus, my Savior, and my King
He picked me up off the ground
And swung me around in his arms
And told me he loved me
Tears started coming down my face
I knew I needed help
And it was the only open door
As help to me
Once I met this man
I quickly took Him and his truth to heart
So I said yes
To Him being my friend, my father, and my savior
Since that day
Life hasn't been perfect
But it has given me a notion
That if all else fails
I still have one true friend
Sometimes I want to give up
But knowing that without him I'd be dead
I cling to his word and his promises that will be there until the end
It's hard at times to be thankful
But in this case
I'm thankful that I will always have a
Father and a friend

Forgiven

My child you are forgiven
I am here now with you
And I want to be with you
For all those times you were searching
I was there
For all those times you cried
I was there
For all those times you gave up
I was there
My daughter I am always here
Beside you
Ready to take you in my arms
To dance a dance with you
I am here to comfort you
Those tears that you hold so dear
It's okay my child
Let them out
I will bear your pain
And I will be your friend
At no expense
Here I am my daughter
Reach out take hold
I will never let you down
Or leave you
I will always love you
My child, you are forgiven
The cross is near
Please lay it down to me, dear child
It's okay

Hallelujah Freedom Is my Friend

It's like they leave you in the shadows
Of yesterday's life
You say that you have moved on
But no one can believe that you have

You're still trekking down the street
With the same old set of crutches
You're still singing your praise to the king
You're still holding on with everything

Jesus today is the day
Where you broke the chains
And set my feet
On wide open ground
Where I could sing
Hallelujah I am free

No more of yesterday
No more crutches
No more chains
I can walk
And shout amen
And claim your freedom

Section VII Friendship

Proverbs 18:24
There are "friends" who destroy each other, but a real friend sticks closer than a brother. (NLT)

A Friend

A friend is someone who is there for you
Someone who respects you as a person
A friend is someone who is always
Filling your day with boosters
But not put-downs

*This is the first poem I ever wrote

Friends until the End

Friends are people
Who are there for you?
When you are in pain
When you need to laugh
Or need to cry

These are the people
Who will be your friends
From dusk until dawn
Every hour in every day
Every day in every year
These are the people who will be
Your friends until the end

Friendships

Things don't always last forever to the world
Some even believe that not all things are possible
But with God all things are possible
Including those ever-lasting friendships

They're the kind
That mean more than anything in the world
Friends are people who are stuck together
Like super glue

They're there for each other
Day in and day out
When one is in need
They try to help them, but if they can't
They pray and simply share their faith with them
When one is down in the dumps
They simply try to cheer them up
When one is sick
They're there for them
When one is out of the loop
They're there to give them advice and encouragement

More than advice, prayer, and
Being there for each other
True friends love each other
With God's love

Saying I Love You

He closed my eyes
So I couldn't see
He took my hand
And got on his knees
Only to say he loved me

He whispered in my ear
Three solemn words
That I thought I'd never hear

I cried just a little
But I realized those words were meant
For me to hear

I have to admit
It's been years since anyone
Has said I love you

My eyes opened
And the world came to me at a glimpse
I suddenly realized
That love is more than a word
But it's a friendship in hand
It's a father telling his child
That everything is going to be okay
That everything is going to work out in the end

My Child

I knew the kind of person
You would be before you were even born
I knew the number of hairs on your head
Even how far you would go in life
For I know your destiny
I've known it forever
Before you even began to discover it
I knew when you would come to me
For I know everything
I am your king

Counselor

God is our counselor
The answers are in his word
So when you're in trouble
Don't run away
But instead stay and seek the Lord
Dig down deep in his word
It's all in there
Everything God wants you to know and more
Trust in the Lord
He will keep you safe
He will be your shield of protection over you
Take that frown and turn it around
Don't hold it all in anymore
Just give it to God
Don't let the pain eat you up inside anymore
Just seek him
After all he is your counselor

Our Father Is All Around

If you think that you have lost everything
Think again
There's someone who will always be there
To love you
To hold you
To be with you
This being is your heavenly father
He will always be there forever
If you look up and around
He is there in the midst
To love on you
To hold you
To be with you
Just look up and around
He is there
He is everywhere

The Greatest Gift Of All

There were times that I struggled in life
But you were there to hold me up
To help me through the hard times
When I fell down
You picked me up
When everyone else abandoned me
You wrapped me in your arms
And held me close
You showed me that you loved me time and time again
You never held my mistakes against me
Rather you showed me grace and forgiveness
And life with the cross

The Man Who Sits Everywhere

I look up to the mountain
Off in the distance
I see a shadow
It's a the shadow of a friend
My helping hand in times of trouble
There is this man I know
His name is Jesus
When I am alone
All I have to do
Is look up and over
He is always there
To help in times of despair
Hue is always there to hold me
In his hands
And to tell me that he loves me

Yesterday's Mark

I keep thinking about yesterday
When you set me free
And I turned around and walked out that door
With a smile on my face
A peace in my heart
A song of joy on my lips

I keep thinking about yesterday
The sorrows of the morning
And the joys of the evening

I keep thinking about yesterday
When you set me free
When you sat down beside me
Only to tell me that you loved me

I keep thinking about yesterday
When I cried the ocean blue
Only to have you set me free

Section VIII Random Poetry

Psalm 69:32
The poor will see and be glad—you who seek God, may your hearts live! (NIV)

Mark 16:15
He said to them, "Go into all the world and preach the good news to all creation. (NIV)

Philippians 2:10
That at the name of Jesus every knee should bow, in heaven and on earth and under the earth. (NIV)

Days of Relevance

I used to think of yesterday
And the days when I was
Bound in the land of Egypt

I used to think of yesterday
And the day when
My struggles were such a torment to me

I used to think of yesterday
And the days when
My voice was irrelevant

Now I see that yesterday
Is a moment in the past
My life then; is nothing like it is now

Today I see each day as a new day
A time of freedom
From every chain or bondage
From the torments of my life
From the voices and words people have instilled into my life

I'm a child of the most high
And my freedom is in him
For peace is like a river that flows endlessly
And Freedom is peace

Heaven's in the sky

Heaven's in the sky
Where all the angels live
This is where the color white
Covers the land

Heaven's in the sky
Clouds of dust
Going in all directions

Heaven's in the sky
Where God the Father lives
Him all dressed in his best
For a celebration of new life

Heaven's in the sky
Having songs and peaceful sediments
To every hearing ear

Heaven's in the sky
Making all in comfort
Of ear new home

Heaven's in the sky
Making home sweet home

Printed in the United States
95686LV00005B/172/A